Dealing with Challenges

Struggling at School

By Meg Gaertner

www.littlebluehousebooks.com

Little Blue House is distributed by North Star Editions:
sales@northstareditions.com | 888-417-0195

Produced for Little Blue House by Red Line Editorial.

Photographs ©: Shutterstock Images, cover, 8, 11, 12, 15, 19, 21, 23, 24 (top right), 24 (bottom right); iStockphoto, 4, 7, 17, 24 (top left), 24 (bottom left)

Library of Congress Control Number: 2021916792

ISBN
978-1-64619-488-9 (hardcover)
978-1-64619-515-2 (paperback)
978-1-64619-567-1 (ebook pdf)
978-1-64619-542-8 (hosted ebook)

Printed in the United States of America
Mankato, MN
012022

About the Author

Meg Gaertner enjoys reading, writing, dancing, and being outside. She lives in Minnesota.

Table of Contents

Struggling at School **5**

Learning Differences **9**

Getting Help **13**

Glossary **24**

Index **24**

Struggling at School

A girl struggles to understand a lesson.

She gets a bad grade on

her homework.

A boy struggles to pay attention in class.

He worries he's not as smart as the other students.

Learning Differences

Struggling at school does not mean you aren't smart.

Everyone learns differently.

You can find your own way
to success.
Many people can help you find
the ways you learn best.

Getting Help

Talk to your teacher and school counselor.

They want you to do well in school.

Teachers can help you understand a tricky lesson. They can teach you skills to succeed at school.

teacher

School counselors are there
to listen.

They can see what is making
school hard.

They can work with you to make
school easier.

school counselor

An adult at home can help you use your time wisely.
He or she can help you study and do homework.

A tutor can meet with you after school.

This person can help you with a specific class.

Everyone needs help sometimes.

It's okay to ask for help.

You can gain the tools to

succeed at school.

Glossary

grade

teacher

school counselor

tutor

Index

C
class, 6, 20

G
grade, 5

L
lesson, 5, 14

T
teacher, 13–14